Nonmonogamy and Happiness

ALSO BY CARRIE JENKINS

MORE THAN TWO ESSENTIALS

Nonmonogamy and
Happiness

Carrie Jenkins

THORNAPPLE
PRESS

Nonmonogamy and Happiness
A More Than Two Essentials Guide

Copyright ©2023 by Caroline Susanne Jenkins

Thornapple Press
300 – 722 Cormorant Street
Victoria, BC v8w 1p8 Canada
press@thornapplepress.ca

Thornapple Press is a brand of Talk Science to Me
Communications Inc. and the successor to Thorntree Press.
Our business offices are located in the traditional, ancestral
and unceded territories of the ləkʷəŋən and W̱SÁNEĆ peoples.

Cover and interior design by Jeff Werner
Cover image generated with assistance from WOMBO
Substantive editing by Andrea Zanin
Copy-editing by Hazel Boydell
Proofreading by Alison Whyte

Library and Archives Canada Cataloguing in Publication
Title: Nonmonogamy and happiness / Carrie Jenkins.
Names: Jenkins, Carrie, author.
Description: Series statement: More than two essentials ; 5
Identifiers: Canadiana (print) 20230528287 | Canadiana (ebook)
    20230528384 | ISBN 9781990869167 (softcover) |
    ISBN 9781990869174 (EPUB)
Subjects: LCSH: Non-monogamous relationships. | LCSH: Love. |
    LCSH: Happiness.
Classification: LCC HQ980 .J46 2023 | DDC 306.84/23—dc23

10 9 8 7 6 5 4 3 2 1

Printed in Canada.

Am Robin, fy nghalon a fy nghartref.

Contents

Acknowledgements

I wrote these words on the traditional, ancestral and unceded territories of the Sḵwx̱wú7mesh (Squamish), səl̓ilwətaʔɬ (Tsleil-Waututh), and xʷməθkʷəy̓əm (Musqueam) First Nations (in what is known colonially as Vancouver, British Columbia). I acknowledge my indebtedness, as an uninvited settler, to those who have cared for this land and these waters for millennia, and my responsibility to support that ongoing work.

I am Welsh, with ancestry from the Gower coast. I spent my childhood in a very rural area of Pembrokeshire, which occupies the furthest southwesterly tip of Wales, near a tiny village called Croesgoch. In Welsh, we say "tra môr yn fur i'r bur hoff bau, o bydded i'r hen iaith barhau." These lines (from our national anthem) mean "as long as the sea is a wall to the pure and beloved land, may the old language [i.e., Welsh] survive."

Wales was conquered by England in the thirteenth century, and there have been efforts to eradicate the old language in favour of English, particularly during the nineteenth century, when speaking Welsh was blamed for endemic poverty and associated with low moral character. Children were ridiculed for speaking Welsh in school, and anyone caught doing so was made to wear a wooden block called a "Welsh not" around their neck. This would then be passed along to the next child caught speaking Welsh, with punishment meted out to whoever was left wearing the "not" at the end of the day.

These measures did not succeed in their object. In fact, Welsh is the only member of a family of old Celtic languages from in and around what is now called the United Kingdom that is *not* currently considered extinct or endangered on account of having been replaced by English.

Boed i'r holl hen ieithoedd ar yr arfordir hardd hwn hefyd barhau.

Introduction

I'm an author and philosophy professor who is fascinated by romantic love. I've been thinking about it for the last decade of my life, during which time my career has been more or less taken over by the subject.

I'VE WRITTEN ESSAYS, POETRY, academic papers and two books on it, but I still feel like there is so much more to say and so much work left to do.

In this book, I'm going to muster some of the ideas about romantic love I've been developing so far—many of which I can now articulate with added perspective—and bring them to bear on the question of what nonmonogamy has (or hasn't) got to do with happiness. My starting point is that a *romantic ideology* plays a central role in our dominant culture. This ideology normalizes the idea that in order to be "happy ever after" (i.e., live a successful life) we must find a partner—"the one"—and form a permanent, monogamous, nuclear-family-type relationship with that person. In so doing, the romantic ideology teaches us that (a) happiness is a very valuable life goal, and (b) achieving it is largely about finding that one particular kind of monogamous romantic love.

In this ideology, romantic love and happiness are positioned as the twin goals of a good life. They are seen as *noble* life goals (unlike, say, money or fame or power). And there's the additional caveat that the one depends on the other: romantic success *is* the way to be happy. In short, then happiness is what you're supposed to want out of life, and conventional, monogamous, romantic love is how you're supposed to go about getting it.

So where does this leave everyone else? In particular, where does it leave those who choose nonmonogamy? Are they just doomed to be miserable? In my humble opinion the answer to that question is no. But—to me—it is much more interesting to consider *what's gone wrong with the question*. The work represented in this book sees me diving further below the waves of these issues than I have gone before and surfacing with a new angle on love and life. This has helped me move through some of the most challenging transitions in my life so far, including the end of a marriage, a shift from polyamory to monogamy, and a wholescale reassessment of my self-image as a "philosophy professor." What's helping me connect these seemingly disparate puzzle pieces turns out to be an old (*very* old) piece of wisdom about the interconnected nature of all things and the dangers inherent in certain kinds of artificially imposed division and separation.

But to explain what that has to do with nonmonogamy and happiness, I'll need to start by gathering some of the fruits of my previous work.

What's the Point?

Whether we're in the midst of an existential crisis, laid low by depression or just awestruck by the vastness of a clear night sky, most of us have at one time or another asked ourselves: *what is the meaning of life?*

WHY ARE WE HERE? WHAT ARE WE supposed to *do* with this mortal existence that none of us asked for but we all now have to deal with? What, in other words, is a life *for*? What is the *point* of it? Some of us feel like we find answers in these moments, and some of us don't. Some of us spend a good deal of time with the questions: probing them, worrying over them and letting ourselves fall deeply into them. Others snap quite quickly and easily back to their everyday concerns. But, at least for a short while, most of us have experienced this kind of curiosity.

The last year of my life has been challenging. Coming out of a marriage is never easy, and although this one ended as kindly and calmly as I could ever have hoped, the process has sometimes left me feeling like I'm in free-fall, as if the question of who and what I am is entirely up for grabs. What is the point of *me*?

This isn't an entirely new experience. For the last 10 years or so, I've been falling more and more deeply into a slightly different kind of question, but one that turns out to have quite a lot in common with questions about the meaning of life. I've been asking myself: what is the meaning of love? What is love for? What's the *point* of love? Fewer people ask these questions, but I think they deserve a lot more air time than they get.

I am especially captivated by what is known as "romantic" love. I believe that every kind of love is valuable and important, and my special interest in romantic love isn't based on any assumption to the effect that it's the *most* valuable or important kind of love. If anything, it's quite the opposite: it's that I'm particularly *troubled* by romantic love and the value placed upon it. I find it confusing, fascinating and sometimes scary.

I'm troubled for political reasons, and for personal reasons. I'm also profoundly *philosophically* troubled by romantic love. And these things overlap: the personal is political, and it's philosophical too. We can't pretend to start from a neutral place when it comes to philosophizing about love.

I started precisely because I realised that my personal experiences were way out of line with what was considered normal and acceptable. By then, I'd started living in nonmonogamous relationships, and talking openly about them. So I'd started hearing all sorts of moral criticisms levelled against me for my nonmonogamy. That was fairly predictable. But I was also hearing, over and over again, that what I felt for my partners was "not real love," because if I was *really* in love, I wouldn't have romantic feelings for anyone else. And once we're arguing about what is or is not "real" love, we are in philosophical territory.

One of my first research articles on the philosophy of love, back in 2015, was about exactly this.[1] It wasn't concerned with the morality of nonmonogamy, but with whether it was even *possible* to be in love with more than one person at the same time. In the philosophy of love that I was reading at that time, there was a general background assumption that romantic love has to be monogamous. But I wasn't finding any good arguments as to *why* it has to be that way. The same year, I published another article surveying a range of different philosophical theories of what love is (romantic love, specifically).[2] Here, I was hoping to find a convincing general theory that could deliver an answer to the question of whether nonmonogamous love is possible or not. I didn't.

But I did find a way of thinking about love that seemed more promising to me than the others on offer, and that sent me in the direction of the theory that evolved into my first book on love, *What Love Is: And What It Could Be*.[3] Even after writing the whole book, I didn't have a clear-cut answer as to whether it's possible to be in love with more than one person at the same time. But I knew a lot more about why the question was so challenging.

To explain, I'll briefly recap the theory from *What Love Is*. The key idea is that romantic love has a dual nature. It is in part biological, and as such, it consists of multipurpose neurochemical mechanisms that are shared with other states. (Chemicals like dopamine and oxytocin, for example, are involved in experiences of reward and of attachment, whether those experiences are of a romantic nature or not.) Considered as a natural biological phenomenon, romantic love can be studied using science, and has ancient evolutionary origins. (That said, it's important not to treat these in a simplistic manner that reflects contemporary cultural biases more than actual evidence.)

But romantic love is not wholly biological. It is also, in part, socially constructed. It is partly composed of things like *scripts* and *norms*. It is, in this sense, "made up," but not in the way that Sherlock Holmes is "made up." It's more like how the law is "made up": it's a social construct, for sure, but it's absolutely real and you'd better pay attention to how it works. The socially constructed side of romantic love is partly constituted by the love stories that we tell—both fictional stories and real-life accounts—and partly by with the complex and ever-changing expectations we place on our own and each other's romantic lives.

These social scripts and norms do a lot of work in determining what makes certain kinds of love count as *romantic*. While all kinds of love have certain features in common—like respect, trust and care[4]—we typically expect romantic love to be *exclusive* (which distinguishes it from familial love or the love of friends), and we *sexualize* romantic love. No other kind of love is *normatively* sexual (despite the fact that people can—and do—maintain loving friendships that include sexual intimacy without being romantically involved.)

I came to the conclusion that some of the hardest philosophical questions about romantic love arise from confusion about how love's biological mechanisms are related to its socially constructed scripts and norms. I ended up theorizing that it's like an actor playing a role: ancient biological mechanisms are asked to perform "romantic love" by conforming to certain scripts. So my question in *What Love Is* became: how good is this casting decision?

It seemed to me that this is something we should expect to be highly variable between people: as a species, one distinctive thing about humans is their capacity for infinite variety. But normative compulsion to conform to a monogamous script strips us of the freedom to *choose* monogamy, which undermines its value even in cases where it would be a good fit for the individuals involved. To choose monogamy, one must choose it freely, not under duress.

The reason this complicates the question of whether it's possible to romantically love more than one person at a time is that we seem to get two different answers from the two halves of love's dual nature. The social script excludes nonmonogamous love from being a genuine form of romantic love: the dominant social norms for romance are very clear that the nonmonogamous person's experiences don't count as "really" being in love. (That's what all those comments were reinforcing for me.) But from a biological point of view, what's going on inside a person who is experiencing intense romantic love with more than one partner might be just the same as what's going on inside someone who is experiencing "normal" monogamous romantic love. (More—and better—science would be needed to confirm this, but I can testify that the two cases can certainly feel quite similar from the inside.) So nonmonogamous love might well turn out to be a "yes and no" case of romantic love. The biology says yes, but the social norms say no.

In this kind of situation, we are faced with a few options for resistance and activism on behalf of nonmonogamous love. Option 1 is to say *who cares about social norms!* They're just made up, after all. We can live how we choose. The problem with this option is it's too close to saying *who cares about the law!* It, too, is just made up, but that doesn't mean we can live how we choose. Policing—whether literal or social—tends to catch up with those who are perceived as breaking society's codes. Nonmonogamous people reasonably fear losing friends, respect and even their jobs and kids if they are open about their relationships. Moreover, those who are already stigmatized or marginalized for other reasons are more likely to be subject to penalties for contravening expectations around their romantic relationships. It's relatively safe (if not necessarily always a fun experience) for me, as a white, middle-class, tenured university professor living in Vancouver, to talk about being in nonmonogamous relationships. It's a lot less safe for someone in a repressive social context such as Iran, Saudi Arabia or parts of the United States. This is especially true if they have other demographic features that make nonmonogamy particularly dicey for them, or if they are dependent on a job with a conservative employer.[5]

Social norms may be "made up," but their consequences are tangible.

Option 2 is to reclaim the script. We certainly need to do this. We need to tell more diverse, and better, love stories. Research and education can help reduce the stigmas and silences surrounding nonmonogamous love, but *representation* is at least as important as either of these things. By telling a wider variety of love stories, both from our real lives and from our creative fictional imaginations, we can challenge the assumption that romantic love always looks like the end of a stereotypical boy-meets-girl rom-com. Representations of nonmonogamous romance, along with other counter-normative forms of love (such as queer and asexual love), will slowly but surely change the scripts and expectations that constitute the socially constructed aspect of romantic love.

Option 2 is the one I advocated for most centrally in *What Love Is*, and I still think it's an important part of the work that remains to be done. But lately I find myself focusing on a third option: to *dethrone* romantic love. By pushing on the question of why romance is such a big deal in the first place, we may discover that what is valuable about romantic love is actually shared by love in *all* its forms, and that romantic love deserves no special place in our value system. Note that this isn't the same thing as defying romantic norms, as per option 1. David may be defiant in the face of Goliath, but he doesn't deny that Goliath is (pardon the pun) a big deal. Option 3 isn't simply defiant, it denies that romance is a big deal. Instead of David facing Goliath, option 3 is more like Dorothy pointing out that the great and powerful Wizard of Oz is in fact a little man behind a curtain.

In my second book on love, *Sad Love: Romance and the Search for Meaning*, I argued that the little man behind the curtain in our analogy is the capitalist, white supremacist patriarchy. It is within and because of this ideology that romance assumes an illusory inflated importance. And the curtain—the smokescreen that conceals this reality—is what's known as *amatonormativity*.

This term was coined by a contemporary philosopher, Elizabeth Brake, to describe the assumption that a certain kind of romantic relationship is what everyone wants (or should want).[6] The amatonormative relationship is an exclusive, permanent, sexual relationship between two people, and it is supposed to be the most important relationship in their lives, taking precedence over any connections to friends, family or community. Amatonormativity is similar to its cousin heteronormativity, insofar as both are structural assumptions about how to love (and how to live) that fly largely under the radar until someone points them out. And insofar as pointing them out doesn't always make you a lot of friends.

Ever since I was old enough to understand a fairy tale, I've understood that the romantic "happy ever after" is what I am supposed to be aiming my life towards. But coming into writing *Sad Love*, I started to ask what love and happiness really have to do with one another. I was living with depression at the time, and questioning whether my inability to experience happiness meant that I was unable to love and be loved. I still thought I was in love—I was in two loving relationships then, and considered myself to be in love with both my partners. But I could not be happy *at all*, never mind ever after. So, I found myself asking, did that mean my love was defective in some way? Was it, after all, not "real" love—not on account of being nonmonogamous, but on account of it not making me happy?

In the course of working on *Sad Love* I realized that in the dominant culture we are all swimming in, amatonormative love is positioned as one of the two main goals of a good life. As I put it earlier, happiness is what you're supposed to want out of your life, and conventional romantic love is how you're supposed to go about getting it.

This means that one really effective way of warning people away from nonmonogamy is to tell them "that will make you miserable." Of course, this strategy of wielding sadness as a big stick to discourage us from doing something isn't specific to nonmonogamy; it can be used for anything people don't want you to do. And on the flipside, happiness can always be dangled as a carrot to encourage whatever people *do* want you to do. As Sara Ahmed powerfully argues in *The Promise of Happiness*, happiness is "used to redescribe social norms as social goods."[7] She writes:

Feminist critiques of "the happy housewife," black critiques of the myth of "the happy slave," and queer critiques of the sentimentalization of heterosexuality as "domestic bliss" have taught me most about happiness and the very terms of its appeal.

A culture's dominant narratives about what makes people happy and what makes them sad are a clear barometer of what that culture values.

Obviously, we can challenge those narratives. But we can also take our questioning to a deeper level by asking what exactly is so terrible about being sad. And, for that matter, what's so great about being happy? What do either of them have to do with whether you're in love or not? These are big questions, and I'm going take a shot at explaining my take on them in the next section. As you'll see, I think sadness—and the other "negative" emotions—are far from being the Big Bad Wolves they're made out to be.

Manifesting Ideology

Saying things like "nonmonogamy will make you miserable," or "you'll never be happy in that kind of relationship," is not only a good way to scare someone off trying, it can also be a self-fulfilling prophecy.

HAVING PEOPLE YOU CARE ABOUT (and random people on the internet) constantly telling you that you're making a terrible mistake can, in and of itself, make you miserable.

More generally, seeing that your friends or family obviously don't support your relationships can be a contributing factor in relationship instability and breakups.[8]

What's worse, once these kinds of messages are seeded in our minds, any nonmonogamous relationships that turn out to be "failures" or "bad" relationships can be taken as evidence that the naysayers were right all along. There's a tendency to blame the nonmonogamy whenever a nonmonogamous relationship doesn't work out, whereas we rarely see monogamy take the hit when a monogamous relationship breaks down. Nobody tells a monogamous divorcée that "monogamy will only make her miserable" and cites her recent divorce as evidence. On the contrary, they tell her to get back out there and keep working on finding "the one." Obviously, the person they just ended things with wasn't "the one," but the idea that there *is* a "the one" always seems to survive intact.

Moreover, it's not only nonmonogamous breakups that are held to this kind of double standard. *Any* kind of emotional "failure" experienced by someone in a nonmonogamous relationship can, with a little effort, be chalked up to their nonmonogamy. A while after I first started talking openly about being in polyamorous relationships, I mentioned online that I also had an anxiety disorder, and a member of my extended family told me that my anxiety was due to having strayed from Jesus with my polyamorous lifestyle.

Leaving Jesus out of this for a second, might it have been fair for her to suspect that my anxiety was caused by my nonmonogamous relationships? I am inclined to doubt it, because I've had issues with anxiety since I was a teenager and I didn't start practicing polyamory until I was over thirty. (She didn't know this, but then again she hadn't bothered to find out.) In any case, whether it was or wasn't is probably a question better left to therapists than to fundamentalist in-laws. But what's interesting to me is that without knowing anything about its nature or its causes, this family member was ready—some might say *eager*—to attribute my difficulties with "negative" emotions to my nonmonogamy.

With the benefit of hindsight, I would say that my nonmonogamous relationships were far from being the cause of my difficulties. They were, on the contrary, my main source of support and strength. (There's always something to be said for having more than one person looking out for you when you find yourself in need of support, whether they're friends, family members or partners.) But there is a bit more going on in this kind of dynamic than a simple mistake about what caused what.

Let me start by explaining why I have been putting scare quotes around the words "negative" and "failure" here. It's because I don't think things like anxiety or sadness, or even breakups for that matter, are necessarily negative things or failures. Take breakups, for starters. (Let's begin with endings!) Many relationships end without being "failed" relationships, simply because they have run their course. Sometimes romantic relationships end because it's the right time for them to transition into other kinds of friendships or chosen-family bonds. Other times, a relationship can end because one partner is escaping abuse at the hands of the other. In this case, the relationship might in some sense be a "failure," but not because it *ended*. Actually, the ending is probably the most positive part of that situation.

And what of the so-called "negative" emotions? Well, I contend that feelings like sadness, anxiety and anger are important and should not be regarded as undesirable or as something to try and eradicate from our lives. Consider anxiety, for example. An anxiety disorder, by definition, is something that is creating a problem, but anxiety itself is not necessarily a negative thing per se. It can be unpleasant, but it can also be valuable—even life-saving—when it accurately alerts us to danger. In fact, I think this is even true of my anxiety disorder. It's now thankfully much less severe than it used to be, but even back when it was creating more serious problems for me, I suspect that it was in fact an adaptive response to an unhealthy situation. I was stressed and distressed by my academic career and working conditions, in ways that I had yet to unpack or understand, and my emotions were trying to warn me that things needed to change. I am grateful to my anxiety, however unpleasant it felt at the time, for helping me save myself by redefining my relationship to my work and my career goals. Once I could hear what it was trying to say, and took that message seriously, it turned out to be a kind of wisdom. For that reason it was not a negative, all things considered, although it had some negative consequences (including making me feel pretty rough at the time).

But even positive things can have negative consequences in the wrong circumstances. When society reacts with disgust to a loving relationship simply because that relationship doesn't conform to the amatonormative script, or to a person's gender on account of their being assigned a different one at birth, or to someone's sartorial choices on account of their body type, there can be horrible consequences. But that doesn't make any of these things—the relationship, the gender or the clothes— negative. The negative consequences in these situations are properly attributed to other people's prejudices.

That's not to deny there can be genuinely negative experiences with anxiety (or the other "negative" emotions). Then again, it's possible to have genuinely negative experiences with the so-called "positive" emotions, too. To give one mundane kind of example, imagine you're so over-excited about an upcoming event that you can't sleep, although you *need* to sleep in order for the event to go well. In that situation, the excitement—however nice or "positive" a feeling it might be in and of itself—is a problem.

Because happiness is so strongly culturally associated with the amatonormative "happy ever after" relationship model that forms the core of the romantic ideology, nonmonogamous relationships are readily assumed to constitute an emotional failure state. (The same goes for alternatives to the amatonormative model, such as living single.) As a result, not only do nonmonogamous relationships tend to get the blame for any "negative" emotions experienced by those partic- ipating in them—as my anxiety was attributed to my nonmonogamy—but stories of nonmonogamous happiness tend to be disbelieved, erased or simply never told in the first place.

This is connected to the role of representation, which I touched on earlier. If stories of happy nonnormative love begin to be included amongst our stock of cultural reference points, then the amatonormative life model could loosen its grip on us as purportedly the only option for a happy (i.e., good) life. The erasure of nonmonogamous happiness is therefore a crucial part of how the "script" for romance is maintained as normative.

This erasure is achieved through multiple means. First, shame and stigma prevent people from telling their own real-life stories of nonmonogamous love, whether happy or sad. One consequence of social disapproval for

options other than normative monogamous relationships is their concealment,
which in turn strengthens the appearance of there being no other options. If
we can't be honest about our happy
nonmonogamous loves, it will look
from the outside as if such things
don't exist.

Then there is the
lack of representation
in media, both fictional
(movies, TV shows,
novels, etc.) and non-
fictional (news coverage, magazine
articles, etc.). I've long been bothered
by the way any kind of media coverage
of nonmonogamous relationships tends
to home in like a laser on either the
sexual aspects of those relationships
or the "drama" of jealousy, or both.[9]
While I have been happy to talk openly
with media over the years about my

own experiences with nonmonogamy, I've had to explain repeatedly to some interviewers that I will not be sharing information about my sex life. This isn't because sex is shameful, or something that nonmonogamy should distance itself from, but because (a) my sex life is private, and (b) the hyper-sexualization of nonmonogamy in the media reinforces the assumption that all nonmonogamous relationships are casual and not "real" love. To be clear: there's nothing wrong with casual sex. It's just not the same thing as a loving relationship, and where nonmonogamy is concerned those two things always seem to be readily con-flated. Worse, in a social context where many people think there *is* something wrong with casual sex—such as that it's dirty, sinful or simply cheap and meaningless—this conflation is a way to stigmatise nonmonogamous people, as well as an erasure of the genuinely loving relationships they engage in.

Representations of problems with nonmonogamy—typically in the form of jealousy—are relatively common. For years, my only exposure to a nonmonogamous character, in real life or in fiction, came from that episode of *Friends* where a married woman enters into a casual sexual relationship with Chandler while also openly dating several other men. Chandler's friends predict that it won't go well, and of course it doesn't.

It's *happy nonmonogamous love* that gets erased in the media. One striking case of this occurred in a high-profile *New York Times* article in 2017, where polyamorous author Kevin Patterson was photographed with his wife, Antoinette, in a photo that he says "shocked the people in [their] lives," because it was, in the words of one of his friends, "the saddest they've ever seen either of us look."[10] This was a case of what on Wikipedia would be called *multiple issues*: the Pattersons are Black, and what they had spoken with the interviewer about was largely ignored in the final piece, which left the conspicuous inclusion of their (unrepresentatively sad) images smacking of tokenism, as well as constituting an erasure both of Black joy and of happy nonmonogamous love.[11]

When we begin to notice this kind of thing happening, we are taking a first look under the hood at some perpetually grinding social mechanisms, specifically those mechanisms that uphold the amatonormative, monogamous "happy ever after" relationship as the dominant model of a good life. This kind of peek behind the scenes is a first step towards a deep understanding of what *happiness* has to do with the policing of romantic relationships, and with the dominant social status of monogamy.

The next step in this journey comes when we understand that the erasure of nonmonogamous joy isn't a stand-alone phenomenon. It is part of a much bigger picture, and as such it is intimately connected with other strands in the dominant North American culture. Let me say a bit more about this bigger picture, so I can put the next few ideas in perspective.

A central element of the dominant culture—or, for that matter, any culture—is its *ideology*. An ideology is largely composed of values: beliefs about what is good and right, as well as what is normal. But it's well known that, in conjunction with power, these things can and will insert themselves into supposedly neutral or objective areas of enquiry. Back in *What Love Is*, I critiqued some of the "science" behind compulsory monogamy, pointing out the role played by an unexamined ideological commitment to the monogamous norm, and more broadly to the idea that the nuclear family structure is a "normal" arrangement for human life.[12] These things can distort our understanding of both evolutionary history and contemporary neuroscience.

I want to call attention to another function of ideology: one that is perhaps less commonly discussed, but is actually critically important. This is the impact of ideology on the physical conditions in which we live. An ideology, in and of itself, is an abstract and intangible thing comprised of beliefs and values. But in conjunction with power it can and will be *made manifest* in the material world.

One of the clearest explanations of how this works comes from Kim Tallbear, a Dakota scholar and Canada Research Chair at the University of Alberta. In an interview, Tallbear describes how amatonormativity was imposed on Indigenous people during the creation of the settler-colonial state.[13] The colonization of the North American continent by Europeans has never been simply a matter of physically occupying land: it was (and is) an absolutely fundamental part of colonization to import and establish the colonial *ideology* as a baseline. To establish a settler state it is necessary to establish the moral and legal authority to exercise absolute power in the colonial territory. This authority belongs to the abstract realm of ideology, and as such it relies on the entrenchment of a supportive ideology together with the elimination of

any potentially threatening alternatives.
Some of the most obvious manifesta-
tions of this ideological colonization
can be seen in the forcible conversion of
Indigenous people to Christian religious
beliefs, in parallel with the suppression
and (often literal) demonization of
Indigenous beliefs, values, traditional
knowledge systems, arts and cultures,
and life-governing spiritual practices.

As Tallbear explains, the creation
of a settler state involves imposing
colonial ideas about how private
property should be divided, including
the presumption of a normative
monogamous family structure:

The colonists divided up the collective
Indigenous land-base into 160
acre allotments that they gave to the
head of household, which was always
a man, and he could get 80 acres for

his wife and 40 acres for each child.
So here you have this imposition of
heteronormative settler sexuality and
family structure onto the land. All of this
stuff came together so I don't understand
how we can go after blood quantum
and private property without going
after monogamy and marriage.... It has
been made deviant, the fact that our
ancestors engaged in plural marriages,
that they might have had same sex
relations.... It's not only the church
that has done this, the state has told
us this, and science has told us this.

In this way the ideology shapes the
land itself, in parallel with its effect
on family structure. An ideology,
an abstract set of beliefs about
what constitutes a good or normal
life, is made materially manifest in
the division of people into nuclear

families, and the division of land into allotted "family-sized" parcels.

On a larger scale, the role of ideology in establishing the settler state can be seen clearly by considering the Doctrine of Discovery—an ethical and political principle grounded in papal bulls from the fifteenth century—which accorded to European Christians the right to take all land and possessions from non-Christians anywhere in the world, and to "reduce their persons to perpetual slavery."[14] This sense of entitlement is what grounds the very idea of settler-colonial nation states like the United States and Canada.

Of course, it is not part of the origin stories that these countries like to tell about themselves. (As Brian Burkhart puts it: "Welcome to Settler

Colonialism. The first rule of Settler Colonialism is: you do not talk about Settler Colonialism."[15]) But they could not exist without these underlying justifications. In Canada, for example, almost all land supposedly now belongs to the British Crown, including large areas of Indigenous land that were *never ceded to the Crown in any agreement or treaty.* How could this state of affairs possibly be justified, if not by appeal to the Doctrine of Discovery and similar principles?

As an absolutely central part of this process, the settler-colonial society must impose its own ideological commitments concerning marriage, sex and the family. These things are about life and death—the survival and reproduction of generations. And they are also about money, which, under capitalism, is at least as important.

Many philosophers, such as Friedrich Engels and Bertrand Russell, have argued that compulsory monogamy is motivated by the institution of private property and inheritance through the paternal line, with Russell adding that certain strands of Christianity are centrally to blame.[16] As religions go, it's hard to find one more concerned with the relationship between father and son than Christianity, so it is not a coincidence that this belief system dominates in a culture that is so preoccupied with paternity, wealth and status. And as my fundamentalist relative helped make evident to me, Christianity is very much in the driver's seat when it comes to policing monogamy in North America. While these connections between monogamy, religion and the dominant North American culture are ideological, and in a sense *philosophical*, we are all subjected to their impacts in very tangible ways, and on a very personal level.

Returning to Tallbear's discussion, we should pay attention to a connection she draws between the ideological imposition of monogamy and the idea of "blood quantum," which is a colonially imposed genetic criterion to determine who is and is not Indigenous by (supposedly) calculating how much Indigenous "blood" (i.e., genetic ancestry) a person has. This is controversial for many reasons, not least because many Indigenous communities do not determine identity through genetics alone.[17] But Tallbear is absolutely right to emphasize how this focus on genetic inheritance "[goes] hand in hand with … the imposition of monogamy and marriage, solo-marriage not plural marriage like my ancestors had—we were non-monogamist."

It is important to be clear that Indigenous peoples have practiced various approaches to family and raising children. There is no one-size-fits-all solution to the challenges of co-operation, social bonding, and identity, so it would be inappropriate to generalize from what Tallbear says here about her own ancestry to other Indigenous groups. However, what *is* generalizable is the point about how colonial ideology *attempts* the imposition of a one-size-fits-all model, where the "one size" is the amatonormative nuclear family model valorized by European Christian traditions.

Seeing matters in this context is essential when it comes to understanding why the amatonormative assumption that *a certain way of living is the only good way to live* is so deeply and firmly entrenched in places like

Canada and the United States. Here, the colonial ideology is *existentially* critical—without it, Canada and the United States cannot continue to exist, and could never rightfully have existed in the first place—and amatonormative values are an absolutely central part of that ideology.

This point is complemented by philosopher Justin Clardy's work on the weaponization of amatonormativity and compulsory monogamy as tools of anti-Black racism in the United States. In brief, Clardy's contention is that US resistance to nonmonogamy has racist and anti-Black origins, including the treatment of enslaved people as less than human and unfit for ("civilized," white, Christian) monogamous marriage.[18] With slavery playing an essential role in the establishment of the colonial state, the colonial ideology needed ways to exclude both enslaved Black people and Indigenous people from occupying the same moral status as white settlers, and the insistence on a specific, Eurocentric life model as *the only good way to live* played a key part in that ideological exclusion.

This can also help us see why challenges to the dominant ideology (and bear in mind here that in this context simply living a happy counter-normative life constitutes such a challenge) so often provoke responses that seem disproportionately angry and defensive. The repercussions of these challenges go deep, and their consequences ripple out far beyond the question of what someone chooses to do in their own relationships. The dominant ideology of North America—a legacy variant of European Christian traditions—is the ethically flimsy foundation on which Canada and the United States depend for their very existence as political entities. Being as flimsy as it is, its ability to survive in an environment of open-minded discussion and debate is limited. So it is protected by other means: through the suppression of that kind of discussion and debate.

In order to achieve and maintain an *unquestioned* dominance, the colonial ideology must enter into every aspect of our lives, and be reinforced from every direction, but without being noticed as anything substantial. It must seem to be comprised of *obvious truisms*. Those who challenge or reject it must be treated as beyond the pale in one way or another: either evil or crazy. (The same mechanics, in my opinion, help make sense of visceral anti-trans sentiment. The very existence of trans people constitutes a challenge to the simple deterministic understanding of gender that is built into this dominant ideology.)

What does all this have to do with happiness? Well, one of the "truisms" it can feel crazy to challenge is the idea that everyone is naturally and rightfully engaged in a pursuit of happiness. But in *Sad Love* I wanted to challenge that idea, and I started by investigating the possibility that this idea is not a human universal (despite it often being presented that way) but rather something that is specifically located in North American ideology. In fact, for the United States, the pursuit of happiness is a core element of national identity, playing a prominent role in the origin story that it likes to tell about itself (in its "Declaration of Independence"). While Canada may like to imagine itself as very different

from the United States, the cultural
and ideological similarities are in many
ways quite striking, with the crux of
the matter being that both nations are
capitalist, settler-colonial states creating
themselves on Indigenous lands.

Under capitalism, the fundamental
unit of a society is the individual
("consumer"), with the nuclear
family forming a slightly
larger consuming unit
bounded by a—literal or
imagined—white picket fence.
The division of land into 160 acre
allotments mirrors the division of people
into these (amatonormative) units. The
ideological promise of "happy ever
after" resides firmly within such a unit.

In fact, the deeper we get
into this, the clearer it becomes
that *division* is the essence of this
entire ideological apparatus.

Who's Afraid of the "Negative" Emotions?

Through my partner Robin Roberts, I've recently learned the phrase "gina 'waadluxan gud ad kwaagid," which means "everything depends on everything else" in X̱aayda Kil (the Skidegate dialect of the Haida language, emanating from the Pacific Northwest coastal archipelago of Haida Gwaii).

ROBIN IS HAIDA, TS'MSYEN AND SQUAMISH. He's worked as an Indigenous Education Teacher with the Vancouver School Board for many years and has been one of my major influences (as well as sources of support) as I've been working on this book.

The Haida aren't alone in emphasizing the importance of interconnectedness. Similar teachings can be found in many Indigenous languages, such as "heshook-ish tsawalk" ("everything is one" in Nuu-chah-nulth),[19] "namwayut" ("we are all one" in Kwak'wala), nə́ ċaʔmat ct ("we are all one" in Hənq̓əminə̓m̓), and "ankosé" ("everything is connected" in Anishinaabemowin).

In the dominant ideology of capitalist North America, by contrast, it is *problematic* to call too much attention to interconnectedness. Widespread appreciation of our dependence on local ecosystems and the land interferes with the extractive exploitation of these things for financial gain. Similarly, capitalism needs to downplay our complex human interconnectedness and interdependence on one another. Capitalism, in its emphasis on the individual, divides us, just like it divides the land. Bonds beyond the nuclear family—friendship, extended family or community—present a risk factor for disruptions to capitalist competition and productivity. They promote things like collective action, co-operative caretaking (of land and of each other), and nonmonetary exchanges of goods and services. Hence we have downplayed the significance of all these diverse social connections, with such detrimental consequences for public health that in May of 2023 the US Surgeon General issued an advisory warning of an "epidemic of loneliness and isolation."[20]

Focusing its attention instead on individuals and individual responsibility, North American capitalism generates narratives such as the "American Dream," presenting the (palpably false) promise than anyone can "succeed," starting from nothing, simply through their own hard work. And running in parallel to these—if somewhat below the surface—is what I have dubbed the "Emotional Dream," in which happiness is positioned as emotional success, and the emotional equivalent of wealth.[21] We are told that anyone can become emotionally successful by doing enough self-care, practicing gratitude, being a "positive" person and so on. Happiness is also used as a carrot to incentivise living in accordance with the dominant social norms, so we're told that the ultimate way to become truly and permanently happy is by getting ourselves into a monogamous hetero marriage and forming a nuclear family (which, presumably, will naturally happen once we stop being such negative, ungrateful wretches).

One thing about the pursuit of happiness, however, is that it does not work. This is what is known as the Paradox of Happiness: trying to become happy is not the way to become happy. This has been explored by numerous philosophers, social scientists and other writers and thinkers, but my favourite statement of it comes from Viktor Frankl, a psychologist, psychiatrist and concentration camp survivor:[22]

To the European, it is a characteristic of the American culture that, again and again, one is commanded and ordered to "be happy." But *happiness cannot be pursued*; it must ensue.

Until we realize this—and most of us never do—we can keep toiling away at the pursuit of happiness forever. This is great for capitalism, however, because in the process we will be buying lots of items—from BMWs and Rolexes to cheap Amazon trash—that we think will make us happy. (This also won't work.[23]) And because in the Emotional Dream ideology the individual is held responsible for their own emotional success (i.e., happiness), when it doesn't work we can blame individuals for not trying hard enough, just as we can blame poor individuals for not working hard enough to succeed financially (ignoring all structural barriers and the enormously unlevel playing field).

However things are really going, we face constant pressure to *appear* successful in both the financial and emotional realms. Just as one can flaunt BMWs and Rolex watches as evidence of being financially successful, those who would like to appear emotionally successful can post lots of  photos of themselves looking happy on social media, or share all their happy stories but none of their sad ones. Eventually, this leads to the toxic positivity that accompanies and sustains the Emotional Dream ideology. We shame and exclude "complainers," "Debbie Downers" and anyone else who interferes with a "good vibes only" atmosphere.

Ignoring or sidelining "complain-ers" is not only a toxic feature of many social contexts, it also plays a vital role in sustaining dominant ideology. Certain kinds of "negative" emotions—specifically, those caused by non-individualistic factors such as systemic discrimination and structural oppression—cannot be satisfyingly blamed on the "negative" (angry, sad, anxious, etc.) individuals, and in fact may be powerful motivations for collective action. In other words, they spell trouble for capitalism.

The mechanisms that lead to the suppression of these kinds of "negativity" are not limited to the shaming and silencing of our emotional "failures." Systematic erasure and mistrust of those with "negative" perspectives is also prevalent. This is, in fact, how the settler population of North America has remained largely ignorant about the historical and ongoing realities of colonial abuses of power: in order for the settler-colonial state to retain its status as legally and morally acceptable, certain "negative" realities need to be airbrushed out of history.

In Canada, the residential school system is a case in point. During its operation, between 1883 and 1996, Indigenous children were taken from their homes and families by force, and placed in church-run, government-funded institutions where their cultures, languages and community connections were violently suppressed. A key goal of this policy was to strip children of their Indigenous beliefs, cultures and values, and replace them with Christian ones—or in the infamous words of Captain Richard Pratt, to "kill the Indian…and save the man." It is hard to imagine a more explicit attempt at the forcible inculcation of settler ideology into generations of young people.

Many of the children encountered physical, sexual and/or emotional abuse. Thousands died. In 1913, the serving deputy superintendent-general of Indian Affairs Duncan Campbell Scott noted of the early residential schools, "It is quite within the mark to say that fifty per cent of the children who passed through these schools did not live to benefit from the education, which they had received therein." And yet testimony to that effect from survivors of the residential school system has been continuously ignored, disbelieved, and belittled by settler audiences. Why?

Philosophers such as Charles Mills and José Medina have argued that in certain circumstances ignorance can be *active*, and not merely a passive lack of knowledge.[24] As Mills puts it:

Imagine an ignorance that resists. Imagine an ignorance that fights back. Imagine an ignorance militant, aggressive, not to be intimidated, an ignorance that is active, dynamic, that refuses to go quietly—not at all confined to the illiterate and uneducated but propagated at the highest levels of the land, indeed presenting itself unblushingly as knowledge …

Another philosopher, Anna Cook, has built upon this idea to explain specifically how a form of active ignorance which she calls "settler ignorance" accounts for the phenomenon of pervasive ongoing resistance to learning about Canada's real history.[25] Stories that threaten the legitimacy of the dominant culture must be discredited if the status quo is to continue. And so, even as thousands of unmarked graves come to light at the sites of former residential schools, settler denialism persists.

Learning and accepting the truth about colonialism can and will bring on negative emotions, such as sadness and anger. Which brings me back to the question: *who's afraid of the "negative" emotions?* Here I take inspiration from poet-activist Audre Lorde and philosopher Myisha Cherry, both of whom have theorized the so-called "negative" emotion of anger not as something to suppress, nor as a discrediting attribute that means one's arguments can be dismissed, but as motivation for taking action when action is needed: a powerful and indispensable force that we should respect and attend to as such.[26]

So who's afraid of the "negative" emotions? The capitalist status quo is afraid of them. The racist, misogynistic, capitalist settler-colonial North

Amercian states are afraid of them.
Or more accurately, they are afraid
of letting them play their proper
role: not as the Big Bad Wolves in
cautionary tales deployed to scare us
away from non-normative individual
life choices, or as evidence of our
personal failure to realize the Emotional
Dream, but as *messages* for us about
what has gone wrong and what needs
to change. The wisdom contained in
these messages is entirely lost when we
try to shut them out by "focusing on
the positive," or leaning harder into
the "pursuit of happiness," including
the romantic "happy ever after."

In order to access this wisdom, we
must instead acknowledge and respect
the ebbs and flows of our own, and
other people's, "negative" emotions.
Only then we can begin to understand
how these things are connected, not

just to personal choices, but to a much bigger ocean of shifting political, structural, and cultural currents in which *everything depends on everything else.*

I'm biased, of course: my partner is Indigenous. Is *that* why I'm writing about settler-colonial ideology in a book about relationships and happiness?

Well, we're all biased. I've said it before but I'll say again: we all bring our own baggage to the table in these discussions (whether or not we acknowledge it). Being considered "normal"—being monogamous, for example—doesn't mean that you're bias-free, although it may mean that your biases are less likely to be regarded as such. If my partner were a white settler like me, would that make me *less* biased?

Here's another way of looking at things: maybe it's not just because I happen to love this person that I see these connections between colonial ideology and the "happy ever after" romantic myth. Maybe the explanation goes the other way around: I'm able to find value and connection in a relationship with someone whose values and whose ways of making sense of the world resonate with my own, someone with whom I can share a sense of purpose and meaning in life.

But I'm getting ahead of myself. The meaning of life, and what it has to do with love and happiness, is the topic of the next section.

A Series of Fascinating Transitions

Half-jokingly (but half-seriously),
I wrote this dedication for my
2017 book *What Love Is*:

> For philosophy with love.
> PS: we need to talk.

PHILOSOPHY AND I WERE, BY THIS TIME,
in a complicated and deeply
troubled relationship, and frankly
I was thinking of ending things.

It had all started out so promisingly.
I was very young, just in my late teens,

when I was first formally introduced to the discipline of philosophy, although it felt as if we'd always known each other. I was in love from the very start, and as a rosy-eyed eighteen-year-old off to university I was already telling everyone that philosophy was my subject, the one for me, and that it would be that way for the rest of my life. I wanted a career in philosophy and I was doing everything I could to make that happen.

I wanted to be a philosopher because I thought that was a way to be able to think about *everything*. I didn't want anything to be off limits, or off my radar as a possible subject of research. I loved the idea of having that complete freedom to move between topics, and to work towards understanding how seemingly disparate things are connected.

I mentioned earlier that the interconnectedness of all things is a theme in

Indigenous thought. It has also made a few appearances in the traditions of thought in which European (and, by extension, North American) culture is rooted. One such appearance is in the work of an ancient Alexandrian alchemist and scientist who is now little-known (perhaps on account of being a woman) and few of whose works survive. She is known as "Cleopatra the alchemist," and a seventeenth-century text credits her with being one of only four women capable of making the philosopher's stone—the substance reputedly able to transmute metals.[27] Her most famous surviving text is her *Chrysopoeia* (gold-making instructions), which includes one of the earliest known alchemical diagrams of a snake eating its own tail—an image known as the *ouroboros* in Hermetic traditions. In the centre of Cleopatra's ouroboros she wrote the words: "ἓν τὸ πᾶν," which means "all is one" in ancient Greek.

I have this image tattooed on my chest. I like the image itself, I like its origin story and I like its message. Maybe my fascination with interconnectedness is why I've ended up, as a professor of philosophy, co-authoring a book of poetry with a historian that is framed around the absence of women speakers from Plato's most famous dialogue about love (his *Symposium*) but that is also about mental illness, the medical establishment, pedagogy, abuse, geology, language, numbers, space travel and the Tarot, without any of this feeling strange to me.[28] Maybe it's why it seems natural, to my mind, to scrutinize the "happy ever after" monogamous love myth by drawing out its connections to dominant settler-colonial narratives about what makes for a good and happy life, and how they make themselves manifest in everything from the landscape to our bedrooms.

In any case, at the beginning of my career, as a doctoral student in philosophy, I was intellectually overexcited to be picking up so many new and powerful conceptual tools, and taking on board so much new information about traditions of thought. But over time, I noticed more and more that only certain kinds of things were being included in these conversations. Noticing that fact—and, especially, starting to ask *why*—marked the beginning of the end of something for me.

To cut a long story short, my academic life did not live up to the hopes I had for it. In common with every other aspect of life under capitalism, it turned out to be dominated by the bottom dollar (and by crude proxies for money, like numbers of publications in certain journals that predict future research income, or positions in university rankings that attract fee-paying students). Philosophy turned out to be dominated by white men teaching and reading almost exclusively other white men, the field was rife with sexual harassment and transphobia, and floating behind all of this was the discipline's smug, self-satisfied sense of itself as *very clever and rational* that it seemed to regard as justifying a widespread ignorance of most of the realities of social life, and even most other disciplines in the university. This was never going to work.

Another crushing disappointment came from the fact that academia also didn't facilitate, or even really permit, the kinds of enquiry that feel most natural and important to me. The academy is divided into disciplines, both administratively and intellectually, and all too often, being "interdisciplinary"—having a foot in two disciplines—is enough for people to regard your work with suspicion, as though it signals that you aren't sufficiently committed to or competent in either discipline. You surely can't be a "real" sociologist if you're also an economist, or (god forbid) a physicist. It all feels eerily similar to the social policing of compulsory monogamy, to be honest: you can't "really" love one discipline if you also love another.

The physical landscape of a contemporary university represents the divisions into disciplines. "The sciences," for example, are typically located far away from "the arts," as though the practitioners of each should expect to have nothing to say to one another. The campus in this way makes physically manifest the values and assumptions of the institution, much as (as Kim Tallbear has pointed out) the division of land into nuclear-family-sized parcels manifests the values and assumptions of colonial patriarchy. This active division of knowledge distracts attention from the reality of interconnection.

For multiple reasons, my academic life gave me an anxiety disorder and eventually depression. I felt as if I was in an abusive relationship. In a sense I was—it just wasn't any of my *romantic* relationships that was the problem. It was my relationship with my work. I felt trapped in something that was bad for me, but also felt as if I couldn't leave. I had no other particularly useful skills, I needed the money to pay my bills, and, for me as for many academics, my career had gotten itself closely bound up with identity and my sense of purpose in life. I would be periodically rewarded and incentivised to stay: drip fed with things like research grants, awards, job opportunities, speaking invitations and promotions. These rewards would come in sporadically, between extended periods where my predominant experiences were fear, shame and hate. The pattern of reward and punishment was extremely unpredictable, as many abusers are. Worst of all, I found myself replicating all of this in my interactions with other academics, alternating between suppressing my awareness of the fact and hating myself for it.

One reason the "negative" emotions are so important is that they keep us safe. Among other things, they can be the way we know we need to escape from abusive relationships—not only relationships with other people, but also with our careers, or for that matter with our colonial nation states. If we value our anxiety, anger and sadness—if we listen to them, rather than marginalizing or suppressing them—they can guide us well.

In *Sad Love*, I claimed that being sad isn't evidence that there is something wrong with your romantic relationship, and that happiness isn't the point of love. I emphasized, though, that this doesn't mean you should stay in an abusive relationship that is making you sad. One difference between being a sad person in a loving relationship and a sad person in an abusive relationship is that, while a loving relationship makes space for all your emotions, "positive" or "negative," and supports you through the challenging ones, an abusive relationship typically won't allow space for your "negative" feelings, and instead demands that they be suppressed and silenced.

And indeed, my experiences in academic philosophy often compelled me to pretend that I had no "negative" emotions—or, in fact, any emotions at all. I felt that only my rationality was valuable in professional spaces. And I thought (because I was taught) that the only right response to feeling awful after being aggressively demeaned in a "debate" was to get a thicker skin. These days, I (half-jokingly) call myself "philosophy's crazy ex-girlfriend," calling attention to the way this phrase is used by abusers to describe the women who've escaped them, deriding their "hysterical" overreactions to putatively normal behaviour. I'm casting philosophy, which is already positioned as a hyper-rational and hence male-coded discipline, in the role of my abusive ex-boyfriend.

I am still a philosophy professor, but I am not in love with the academic discipline of philosophy. I'm not invested in it for my identity or for the meaning of my life. I prefer to think of my work these days as undisciplined, a term I prefer to "interdisciplinary," since the latter suggests that one is still acknowledging the disciplinary structure despite straddling some of its divisions.

To make this work, in my professional life I am now engaged in what Jane E. Dutton and Amy Wrzesniewski have called job-crafting: "changing your job to make it more engaging and meaningful."[29] My research is not at all typical for someone in a philosophy department. It involves dialogue with others across various disciplines, and people outside of academia altogether.

It includes creative work: I write in a variety of genres these days, not just the academic monograph and journal article that I was taught were the acceptable forms of scholarly output. Along with poetry, I also write fiction.[30] I regard these as forms of creative research continuous with my non-fiction writing (such as the book you're reading right now).

This kind of job-crafting isn't entirely cost-free—much of my work these days is regarded in certain circles as "not real philosophy" and "not real scholarship"—but I am in a privileged position as a tenured full professor, and I want to use that privilege to expand the range of possibilities that will be available to future generations of scholars. I want to make the case for taking a broader view of what a scholar can be.

To be clear, though, that's not the only reason I'm doing this. It's also simply a matter of trying to make meaning in (and of) my own life. The subtitle of *Sad Love: Romance and the Search for Meaning* is an homage to the standard English title of Viktor Frankl's book *Man's Search for Meaning*. (The book's original title, incidentally, is not gendered: it's simply the German for "A Psychologist Experiences the Concentration Camp"). My early-career experiences of academic life sucked the meaning out of research and scholarship for me. My happiness plummeted as a consequence, and I fell out of love with (the academic discipline of) philosophy. But my "negative" emotions weren't the problem here; they were an accurate and necessary signal that there was a problem.

The flip side of not devaluing the "negative" emotions is not over-valuing the "positive" ones, and I follow Frankl in placing *meaning*, not happiness, at the centre of a good life. In Frankl's terms, happiness cannot be pursued, although it can *en*sue in a life that feels meaningful to the person living it. In *Sad Love*, I was working to resist the romantic ideology "happy ever after" love, and focus attention instead on love that is what I call *eudaimonic*—an Ancient Greek term which literally means "good-spirited." The questions that preoccupied me in *Sad Love* were no longer primarily about what love is or what it could be, but about what it *should* be. What is actually *good* about love? Or—to return to the framing with which I began this booklet—what is the *point* of love?

Eudaimonia, as I came to understand it, is about our interconnectedness, not only with one another, but also with various other kinds of "spirits"—vibes, zeitgeists, movements, climates figurative and literal—that surround us and permeate our lives. Living a "good-spirited" life is a matter of how all of these things interact to create or suppress *meaning* in our lives. A eudaimonic human life is one conducive to collaboration and the co-creation of meaning, in whatever form that may take for the people involved. And this is one of the ways in which humans are strikingly and beautifully diverse: what fills our lives with purpose might be anything from raising children to researching theoretical physics to planting trees to drawing comics.

A eudaimonic *love* is, likewise, one that leads us towards collaborating in those meaning-making activities. In the end, this is why romantic love isn't special and doesn't belong on its pedestal: *any* kind of love can be eudaimonic. Nonmonogamous love may have less claim to being a "romantic" form of love, insofar as "romance" is defined by conformity to certain social norms. But it has every claim to being eudaimonic if it is contributing to making life meaningful for the people involved. Ultimately, my hope is that shifting our focus from romantic love to eudaimonic love can help us appreciate what is truly valuable about love, in all its forms, and to be better able to see and respect that value, whether or not the love conforms to the expected scripts and stories.

For the first time in my life, I have recently found myself choosing monogamous love, and as someone who's been publicly visible for quite a while now as both nonmonogamous and a vocal advocate for nonmonogamous relationships, I keep hearing the theme tune from *Unbreakable Kimmy Schmidt* playing in my head, telling me "that's gonna be a … you know, a … fascinating transition." Honestly, though, I wish it *wasn't* anything to write home about when somebody transitions from monogamy to nonmonogamy or vice versa. In a perfect world, we would normalize these kinds of transitions.

Tailoring one's love life to suit the skills and situations of the people involved is what I have come to call love-crafting. It's named after job-crafting, with which it has a lot in common. Both, I think, are best thought of as ongoing processes, not one-and-done deals. And the more we understand this, the better we can help and support each other through the transitions.

Help is already starting to arrive on the scene, for example in the form of Jessica Fern and David Cooley's book *Polywise,* which is all about transitions from monogamy to nonmonogamy.[31]

As far as my own "notes from the field" go, I can confirm that—as I've long suspected—chosen monogamy feels very different from the unchosen monogamy I experienced in my twenties. It feels intentional and meaningful—eudaimonic in the sense of good-spirited. I've always advocated for chosen monogamy as a valuable relationship status, arguing that it *requires nonmonogamy to be available as well*, since otherwise monogamy is not a choice.

I thought I was making this case for the benefit of other people, but it turns out I was advocating for my future self. One of the reasons I always

advise people to think twice before
sounding off about nonmonogamy
is that you never know who's in the
room: your friends or family might be
in nonmonogamous relationships, and
if you make snide remarks about "those
people" you'll just be making it clear
to them that you're not somebody they
can confide in. But perhaps even more
insidious is the fact that your future
self hears you too. And policing your
future self is a recipe for stagnation.

I have sometimes been tempted to
describe all the shifting and interlocking
dynamics in my career path and my
relationships in Lemony Snicket's
terms, as a series of unfortunate events.
But the reality is that change—even
unsettling and difficult change—is a sign
of life. One of my favourite sayings is
"changing your mind is evidence that
you have one." Relationships, just like

careers, and minds for that matter, are best thought of as living things that change and grow, rather than static entities frozen in time.[32] So I've come to see this period of my life as a series of fascinating transitions. (And as a 44-year-old cis woman, let me tell you I can hardly wait for the hormonal rollercoaster of menopause to kick in.)

Since I have now chosen monogamy, there might be a temptation in certain quarters to say that nonmonogamy didn't work out for me in the end. This would be a mistake: just as the end of a relationship doesn't have to mean the relationship has "failed," a change of relationship type doesn't have to mean that the previous relationship type "didn't work out." On the contrary, nonmonogamy worked out very well for me, for over 10 years. All the relationships I had during those years were great experiences. None of them were failures, and none of them are things I regret. Similarly, choosing monogamy now doesn't mean I was "wrong" about being polyamorous. I *was* polyamorous, and now I'm not.

Does that at least mean that being nonmonogamous is a choice, rather than an identity? Not at all. This is something of a false dichotomy in the first place, because some identities can change (consider social class, for example, or parenthood, or disability). And some identity changes can be undertaken voluntarily (consider religious conversion, or acquiring a new nationality). At most, it means that my preferences changed, based on my situation and the other people involved. (No woman is an island, especially not when it comes to relationships—the other people involved are a rather important factor!) And it doesn't mean that *other* people can or should change.

In short, whether being (non) monogamous constitutes an identity is not the same question as whether it could change, and in any case we shouldn't assume it will be the same for everybody. Being unduly fixated on the question of whether nonmonogamy is an "identity" may be linked to a temptation to *justify* or *excuse* nonmonogamy on the grounds that it is an involuntary and unchangeable condition (because an identity feels more involuntary and unchangeable than a mere preference), and hence the nonmonogamous cannot be blamed for being the way they are. But none of this is necessary. Nonmonogamy requires no excuse of this kind. Identity or not, involuntary or not, there's simply nothing here that needs justification.

Does monogamy make me happier than nonmonogamy? I don't think so, but that's also kind of an irrelevant question for me. Being happy is not the point of my life, and nor is it the point of my loving relationships. A monogamous relationship is—now—part of what's making my life feel meaningful and valuable, and in that sense this monogamous relationship is eudaimonic for me. But I can't emphasize enough that this is the case *because of my specific circumstances*—what is going on in my life, who I'm partnering with, and what I need and want and can offer. All of these things are constantly in flux, and so what makes life, and love, feel right to me is a delicately balanced equation

with constantly shifting variables.
Everything depends on everything else.

But that's how it is with all of us:
each of us sits within their own intricate
web of connections, influences, skills
and desires, interacting in complex ways
that we can't necessarily predict. None
of us knows how our story is going to
end. My hope in sharing these thoughts
with you is that they might support you
in the (lifelong) work of understanding
what that delicate balance looks like
in your own case, and how you can
tilt your own web in the directions
that fill your life with meaning.

None of which requires spending
any more of our time worrying
about whether nonmonogamous
love—or for that matter monogamous
love—can ultimately "make us
happy." That's not the *point* of love.

Notes

1   "Modal monogamy," *Ergo* 2 (8), 2015, pp. 175–94.

2   "What is love? An incomplete map of the metaphysics," *Journal of The American Philosophical Association* 1 (2), 2015, pp. 349–64.

3   New York, Basic Books, 2017.

4   These "ingredients" of love, and others, are detailed by one of my most important philosophical influences, bell hooks, in her book *All About Love: New Visions* (New York, William Morrow, 2000).

5   Justin Clardy has argued, for example, that Black men are subjected to specific social penalties for engaging in consensual nonmonogamy. He describes being told by a formerly close friend that even talking about the subject in an academic context would be "a step back for black people." For details, see his paper "'I don't want to be a playa no more': an exploration of the denigrating effects of 'player' as a stereotype against African American polyamorous men," *Analize – Journal of Gender and Feminist Studies* 11 (25), 2018, pp. 38–60.

6   Elizabeth Brake, *Minimizing Marriage: Marriage, Morality, and the Law* (Oxford, Oxford University Press, 2012). See especially chapter 4.

7   Durham, NC: Duke University Press, 2010. These passages are taken from the Introduction.

8   Besides being intuitively obvious, empirical support for this claim can be found in published research. Examples include Susan Sprecher's "The influence of social networks on romantic relationships: through the lens of the social network" (*Personal Relationships* 18 (4), 2011, pp. 630–44), and her earlier work with Diane Felmlee, "Romantic partners' perceptions of social network attributes with the passage of time and relationship transitions" (*Personal Relationships* 7 (4), 2000, pp. 325–40).

9   I wrote about the first issue back in 2016, in an article for *The Establishment* called "Dear media: polyamory is not all about sex."

10 See his *Huffington Post* article, "The *Times* piece about open marriages doesn't represent my experience," available at: https://www.huffpost.com/entry/how-representation-worksor-doesnt_b_59179e37e4b00ccaae9ea39d.

11 I talk in more detail about this case and related issues in chapter 2 of *Sad Love*.

12 See especially chapter 1.

13　Originally published in Spanish in the Chilean magazine *La Juguera*. The English translation is available at: http://www.criticalpolyamorist.com/homeblog/kim-tallbear-the-polyamorist-that-wants-to-destroy-sex-interview-by-montserrat-madariaga-caro.

14　The bull in which this passage appears is "Inter Caetera," issued in 1493 by Pope Alexander VI.

15　*Indigenizing Philosophy Through the Land: A Trickster Methodology for Decolonizing Environmental Ethics and Indigenous Futures*, East Lansing, Michigan State University Press, 2019, p. 3.

16　See Bertrand Russell's *Marriage and Morals*, originally published in 1929, and Friedrich Engels, *The Origins of the Family, Private Property and the State*, first published in 1884.

17　Tallbear has a helpful discussion of some of the problems with this in her paper "Genomic Articulations of Indigeneity" (*Social Studies of Science* 43 (4), 2013, pp. 509–33).

18　Clardy's book project in progress, titled *Love Hates Us: Love Race and Non-Monogamies in America*, examines this issue. Prior to its publication, some of its central ideas can be found in his talk "Polyamory in Black," presented at the *Philosophy and Non-Monogamies* conference of 2022, available at: https://youtu.be/YP3E_xi6eto.

19 A thorough exposition of the Nuu-chah-nulth philosophy of Tsawalk ("one") can be found in Umeek E. Richard Atleo's book *Tsawalk: a Nuu-chah-nulth Worldview* (Vancouver, BC, University of British Columbia Press, 2004).

20 This document is available at: https://www.hhs.gov/sites/default/files/surgeon-general-social-connection-advisory.pdf.

21 I say more about this in chapter 1 of *Sad Love*.

22 From *Man's Search for Meaning*, first published in German in 1946. This passage comes from p. 137 of the 2006 edition (Boston, MA, Beacon Press). Emphases added.

23 The only way I know of in which it might be possible to "buy happiness" involves buying back your *time*: see for example Whillans et al., "Buying time promotes happiness," *Proceedings of the National Academy of Sciences* 114 (32), 2017, pp. 8523–7.

24 See José Medina, *The Epistemology of Resistance* (Oxford, Oxford University Press, 2012) and Charles Mills, *Black Rights/White Wrongs: The Critique of Racial Liberalism* (Oxford, Oxford University Press, 2017) especially chapter 4, "White Ignorance," in which the quoted passage appears.

25 "Recognizing settler ignorance in the Canadian Truth and Reconciliation Commission," *Feminist Philosophy* Quarterly 4 (4) 2018, pp. 1–25.

26 I highly recommend Audre Lorde's essay "The uses of anger" (*Women's Studies Quarterly* 9 (3), 1981, pp. 7–10) and Myisha Cherry's book *The Case For Rage: Why Anger is Essential to Anti-Racist Struggle* (Oxford, Oxford University Press, 2021).

27 The text is Michael Maier's *Symbola Aureae Mensne Duodecim Nationum*. For details, see Raphael Patai, *The Jewish Alchemists*, Princeton, NJ, Princeton University Press, 1994, p. 78.

28 *Uninvited: Talking Back to Plato*, with Carla Nappi (Montreal, QC, McGill-Queen's University Press, 2020).

29 This phrase comes from their recent *Harvard Business Review* article, here: https://hbr.org/2020/03/what-job-crafting-looks-like.

30 I'm proud of some of it, too. My short story "The Woman at Home" won the *New Philosopher* Writers' Award XXI. My first novel, *Victoria Sees It*, was published in 2021 by Strange Light from Penguin Random House Canada, and was shortlisted for the Frye Academy Award and the Ethel Wilson Fiction Prize.

31 Victoria, BC, Thornapple Press, 2023.

32 See *Sad Love* pp. 57-9 for more on why this is important, and how the romantic ideology's fetishization of *not* changing can be dangerous.

More Than Two Essentials is a series of books by Canadian authors on focused topics in nonmonogamy. It is curated by Eve Rickert, author of *More Than Two: A Practical Guide to Ethical Polyamory* and *Nonomonogamy and Jealousy*. Learn more at morethantwo.ca.

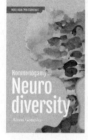

Nonmonogamy and Neurodiversity

Nonmonogamy and Jealousy

Nonmonogamy and Happiness

Nonmonogamy and Death

It's Called Polyamory:
Coming Out About Your
Nonmonogamous Relationships

Tamara Pincus and Rebecca Hiles, with
a foreword by Kendra Holliday

"Doing poly, holding poly space
in the world, is hard work, often
thankless. Thanks to this wonderful
resource, it's now a lot easier."
    — Loraine Hutchins, co-editor, *Bi Any
Other Name: Bisexual People Speak Out*

Ask Yourself: The Consent
Culture Workbook

Kitty Stryker, with a foreword by
Wagatwe Wanjuki

"*Ask: Building Consent Culture*
editor Kitty Stryker invites readers
to delve deeper, with guest experts
and personal anecdotes, to manifest
a culture of consent in one's own
community that starts at the heart."
    — Jiz Lee, editor of *Coming Out
Like a Porn Star*

Ask Me About Polyamory: The Best of Kimchi Cuddles

Tikva Wolf, with a foreword by Sophie Labelle

"The warm and open style, and great way of getting complex things across simply, makes it one of the best relationship comics out there."
— Dr. Meg-John Barker, author of *Rewriting the Rules*

Love's Not Color Blind: Race and Representation in Polyamorous and Other Alternative Communities

Kevin A. Patterson, with a foreword by Ruby Bougie Johnson

"Kevin does amazing work both centering the voices of people of color and educating white folks on privilege. His words will positively influence polyamorous communities for years to come."
—Rebecca Hiles, The Frisky Fairy

Carrie Jenkins is a professor of philosophy at the University of British Columbia and the author of *What Love Is: And What it Could Be* and *Sad Love: Romance and the Search for Meaning*. She holds a PhD in philosophy from Trinity College, Cambridge, and an MFA in creative writing from UBC. She has been featured in *The Atlantic*, the *New York Times*, the *Globe and Mail* and the *Telegraph*, among other publications.